BEAN SPROUTS KITCHEN

simple & creative recipes to spark kids' appetites for healthy food

shannon payette seip *and* kelly parthen

Creators of **beansprouts** café

Photos by Lynn Renee Photography, Shannon Payette Seip, and Amy Lynn Schereck

FAIR WINDS

Brimming with creative inspiration, how-to projects, and useful information to enrich your everyday life, Quarto Knows is a favorite destination for those pursuing their interests and passions. Visit our site and dig deeper with our books into your area of interest: Quarto Creates, Quarto Cooks, Quarto Homes, Quarto Lives, Quarto Drives, Quarto Explores, Quarto Gifts, or Quarto Kids.

First Published in 2018 by Fair Winds Press, an imprint of The Quarto Group, 100 Cummings Center, Suite 265-D, Beverly, MA 01915, USA.
T (978) 282-9590 F (978) 283-2742 QuartoKnows.com

Fair Winds Press titles are also available at discount for retail, wholesale, promotional, and bulk purchase. For details, contact the Special Sales Manager by email at specialsales@quarto.com or by mail at The Quarto Group, Attn: Special Sales Manager, 401 Second Avenue North, Suite 310, Minneapolis, MN 55401, USA.

22 21 20 19 18   1 2 3 4 5

ISBN: 978-1-59233-849-8

Digital edition published in 2018
eISBN: 978-1-63159-548-6

Library of Congress Cataloging-in-Publication Data

Seip, Shannon Payette, author. | Parthen, Kelly, author.
Bean Sprouts kitchen : simple and creative recipes to spark kids'
   appetites for healthy food
ISBN 9781631595486 (e-book) | ISBN 9781592338498 (pbk.)
1. Quick and easy cooking. 2. Children--Nutrition. 3. Bean Sprouts
   (Cafe)
LCC TX833.5 (ebook) | LCC TX833.5 .S453 2018 (print)
   641.5/12--dc23
2018021707 (print) | 2018023069 (ebook)

Design: Kathie Alexander
Page Layout: Megan Jones Design
Photography: Lynn Renee Photography, Shannon Payette Seip, and Amy Lynn Schereck
Illustration: Adrienne Hedger

Printed in China

National praise
for Bean Sprouts:

"Even your picky eater will love this cute food."
—Parenting

"Bean Sprouts is a parent's paradise."
—FastCasual.com's Top 100 Movers & Shakers (multiple award winner)

"Replace ho-hum snacks with fun to eat (and make) treats."
—FamilyFun

"So bright and colorful you'll have kids running to the table."
—Good Morning America

". . . a hip café devoted entirely to kids."
—Everyday with Rachael Ray

". . . ways to get your child excited about nutrition."
—Working Mother

". . . focusing on healthy eating for children."
—New York Times

"Their kid-friendly concept is not only whimsical and healthy but
inclusive of children with food allergies and celiac disease."
—AllerTrain's Best Food Allergy Innovation Award, 2017

CONTENTS

60 recipes inspired by our award-winning kids' menu!

Easy to make and allergy friendly

INTRODUCTION

Drumroll, peas...

Bean Sprouts is the nation's leading kid-focused healthy café chain. We are inside some amazing family destinations, like children's museums, science centers, amusement parks, zoos, and national parks.

© DISCOVERY CUB

Our low kids' counter lets us see our youngest customers!

© SHANNON CORKER PHOTOGRAPHY

Our kids' menu is what stands Bean Sprouts apart from the crowd. With many kids' menus, you see the same boring options: chicken tenders, hamburgers, hot dogs, mac and cheese, etc.— usually as an afterthought in a small section on the back of the menu. We wanted to think outside the lunchbox and create whimsical and imaginative dishes packed with healthy ingredients. We wanted menu items so visually appealing they spark delight and make you chuckle. Bean Sprouts cafés even have a lower counter displaying our menu to empower youngsters to make their own good-for-you choices.

With so many customers asking for our recipes, we are excited to bring you *Bean Sprouts Kitchen*—our whimsical cookbook packed with a behind-the-beans look at what we do, how we do it, and why we do it.

Our Beaneology

We—Shannon "Peacasso" Seip and Kelly "Pea Brain" Parthen—knew firsthand the challenges parents face when eating out with children. Perhaps your son or daughter is like Shannon's son, Isaac, who used to dump every saltshaker out to create "snow" for his trains. Dining out can be messy and stressful. We wanted to create an anxiety-free, guilt-free dining experience, where parents didn't feel like they always had to say no.

We came up with Bean Sprouts—a hip and healthy café that appeals to both kids and adults. We quickly found our niche inside of family destinations, where there was a big need for more wholesome food options.

We landed on the name Bean Sprouts because it's:

- A cute nickname for a kid, and we knew our business would focus on children.

- The name of a healthy food.

- Something that grows, and we wanted a business that would grow and help lots of families.

WHAT'S YOUR BEAN NAME?

Every employee at Bean Sprouts has a "Bean Name"—a nickname that incorporates healthy food. Some of our favorite names: Bean Jovi, Katniss Everbean, and R2Pea2. Post your family's Bean Names to your social media and use the hashtag #beansproutskitchen

FROM LEFT TO RIGHT. BACK ROW: Kelly "Pea Brain," Kale (his real name too), and Shannon "Peacasso" FRONT ROW: Makena "Sweet Pea," Bini "Jumping Bean," and Isaac "MVPea"

Our Ingredients

At Bean Sprouts, and in this book, we follow the guidelines below to make sure kiddos aren't consuming yucky artificial stuff. But, in short: no artificial anything—no artificial flavors, colors, or preservatives—and clean ingredients. Feel free to swap in other foods, but we hope this inspires you to change up a few things in your pantry.

Bean Sprouts is well-known for being allergy-friendly. We can accommodate nearly every dietary need in our cafés. In this book, we did our best to give you flexibility to use whatever milk you like, or substitute plant-based protein for chicken, for example. Additionally, gluten-free flour works wherever you see flour listed.

We also pride ourselves on being Green Beans, using all compostable packaging. In *Bean Sprouts Kitchen*, we encourage you to do the same— for example, try using compostable or reusable straws instead of plastic ones.

beansprouts®

Our PhilosoPEA:

Spark kids' appetites for yummy, good-for-you food; and delight grown-ups with a happier mealtime!

Our food is **clean!**

- No artificial flavors
- No artificial colors
- No artificial preservatives
- No antibiotics
- Allergy-friendly

Our Recipes

In addition to sharing our favorite kids' recipes, we wanted to give you gobs of ideas for wholesome and whimsical entrées and snacks. We hit on what youngsters already love and created recipes around those themes—from race cars and pets to building blocks and tutus.

We also turned to our family destinations—from children's museums to zoos—for inspiration when creating recipes for this book, such as zoo animals, space exhibits, and vintage wooden roller-coasters.

Finally, we listened to what parents ask for in a cookbook—more non-meat proteins and produce packed into playful presentations. So, you'll see that here, too.

How We Create a Kids' Recipe

Sometimes, when we create a recipe, we twist a kid's favorite, classic meal into a more wholesome and playful take. Our Grilledzilla on page 47, for example, is a grilled cheese sandwich, but we play it up with a crazy grin, and give it a healthful boost of veggies with googly eyes made of zucchini rounds and olive slices.

Sometimes we'll come up with a funny name first and then work backwards to see what we can create. Crocamole was a name we had in our pocket for a while. Then, after some recipe tinkering in the Bean Sprouts kitchen, the little guy you see on page 54 was born.

Crocamole!

BEFORE: Plain ol' grilled cheese

AFTER: Grilledzilla!

How to Use this Book

We know that getting kids to try new tastes and eat healthy foods can sometimes be tricky and frustrating. But studies have shown that the more playful an item and the more hands-on your child can be in the process, the more likely he or she is to try something new. With this book in your hands, you've already taken the right first step.

There's no right or wrong way to approach these recipes. The instructions, ingredients, and presentations are meant to spark your imaginations. But if your daughter hates sunglasses, have her give your Wrap Star a baseball cap. We've had kids who didn't want to create sharp carrot teeth for Crocamole and used them for huge eyelashes instead. Be creative! What matters is that your family has fun and tries something new.

On the flip side, it's hard not to feel defeated if your child doesn't like what you make (Shannon's youngest, Bini, would open his mouth, tilt his head down, and let everything fall out dramatically). Though your initial reaction may be to get frustrated, remember this fact: Studies have shown that introducing a child to a new taste may require as many as eight to ten tries before he or she ends up liking it.

So, if your child tries hummus for the first time and doesn't like it, try, try, and try again. This is just a step in the process. And sometimes your child simply won't like a certain food. Remember, you don't like every food in the world either.

We've divided this book into five sections:

- **Eats:** Mostly lunch stuff, with a few dinner-type entrées sprinkled in

- **Nibbles:** Lots of fruits and veggies are packed in this section

- **Sips:** Playful presentations of drinks

- **Breakfast Bites:** Ideas to get you out of the morning rut

- **Treats:** Goodies that have a wholesome twist and are playful in their presentation

We've included a lot of recipes that use child scissors. Of course, you can use regular adult scissors or a knife, but the child scissors are intended for your child to use to help cut shapes, trim ingredients, etc. This is an easy and effective way to empower your child. And, since you know your kids better than anyone, we leave it up to you to decide how much involvement they will have in making these recipes.

You'll also see these special notes:

behind the beans

These are a sprinkle of fun facts about Bean Sprouts throughout this book, giving you the inside scoop on our approach, culture, and history.

bean there, ate that

These are suggestions for changing up the ingredients or new approaches to the recipe.

bean appétit!

You'll see "Bean Appétit!" at the end of every recipe. It's our way of saying "Happy eating!" and what our Bean Team employees say when they present each customer with his food.

Shannon and Kelly hid their children's birthdays within the Bean Counter artwork.

Bean Our Guest

We'd love to see what you create. We encourage you to upload photos of your concoctions to your social media and use the hashtag #beansproutskitchen. For more information about Bean Sprouts and our upcoming locations, visit our website at beansprouts.com.

Peas out!

EATS

From marching meatballs to silly sandwiches,
we've amped up the wholesomeness of mealtime.

SPACEADILLA

Silly shapes of crunchy veggies blast this dish to infinity and beyond.

4 flour tortillas

½ cup (58 g) shredded cheddar cheese

½ cup (113 g) shredded rotisserie chicken

¼ cup (65 g) salsa (optional)

1 tablespoon (15 ml) extra-virgin olive oil

1 small jicama

12 olive slices

1 each red and orange bell pepper

1 can (16-ounce or 455 g) refried black beans, warmed

YOU WILL ALSO NEED:

Child scissors

Mini star and moon cookie cutters

1. Use the child scissors to cut out 8 identical rocket shapes from the tortillas. On 4 of the rocket shapes, evenly divide the shredded cheese and chicken. Top with salsa, if desired, and the remaining tortillas.

2. Heat a large skillet over medium heat and add extra-virgin olive oil. Carefully add the rockets to the skillet. Cook until golden on both sides, about 3 minutes per side.

3. While the rockets are cooking, cut the jicama into thin slices. Use the mini cutters to cut 16 to 20 stars and moons. Use the child scissors to cut flame shapes from orange and red bell peppers.

4. Use the back of a spoon to spread the warmed refried beans across 4 plates. Place a rocket quesadilla in the middle of each plate. Add pepper flames at the bottom of the rocket and olive slices in the center for portholes. Add jicama stars and moons on the refried beans.

Bean appétit!

Makes 4 Spaceadillas

bean there, ate that

What other veggies can you experiment with to create solar systems and planets on your plate?

ROLLER TOASTER

This garlic toast coaster both starts and ends in a splash of yummy tomato soup.

FOR THE SOUP:

¼ cup (55 g) unsalted butter

½ yellow onion, diced

1 can (28 ounce or 794 g) whole peeled tomatoes, undrained

1½ cup (355 ml) water

2 tablespoons (30 g) pesto

¼ cup (60 ml) milk

Salt to taste

½ cup (58 g) your favorite shredded cheese

FOR THE ROLLER TOASTER:

Cooking spray

1 container pizza dough

1 tablespoon (14 g) unsalted butter, melted

1 teaspoon garlic powder

½ teaspoon salt

YOU WILL ALSO NEED:

Muffin tin

Pastry brush (optional)

To make the soup:

1. Melt the butter in a medium pot over medium heat. Add the onion and lightly brown, about 5 to 7 minutes. Add can of tomatoes with juice, water, and pesto and bring to a boil. Reduce to a simmer and cook uncovered for about 40 minutes. Stir occasionally.

2. Remove from heat and let cool slightly. Stir in milk. Puree in small batches in food processor and return to stovetop on simmer until the Roller Toaster is out of the oven.

To make the Roller Toaster:

1. Preheat the oven to 400°F (200°C).

2. Spray the backside of a muffin tin with cooking spray.

3. If your pizza dough is already rolled and flat, cut dough into long strips. If the dough is in a ball, roll the dough to about ¼ inch (6 mm) first, and then cut into strips. Use pastry brush or your finger to brush strips with melted butter. Sprinkle with garlic powder and salt.

4. Weave the strips around the bumps on the bottom side of the muffin tin in whatever Roller Toaster track design you'd like, buttered side facing out (see opposite, bottom).

5. Gently press the dough against the muffin tin bumps to help hold the shape. Bake track side up for 8 to 10 minutes or until the surface is lightly browned. Let cool slightly. Carefully remove from the muffin tin.

6. Divide the soup into 2 bowls. Sprinkle cheese on top. Position your Roller Toaster so each end of the bread dips into a bowl of soup.

Bean appétit!

Serves 2

bean there, ate that

Test the limits of your track by adding as many hills, loops, and drops as your dough (and physics) will allow.

ARMADiLL-YO

This dill-yogurt dipping sauce is no choke—you'll dig it.

FOR THE ARMADILL-YO:

1 artichoke

2 asparagus stalks

8 broccoli stems, about 1 inch (2.5 cm) long

1-inch (2.5 cm) thick slice of cooked chicken or turkey breast

FOR THE DILL-YOGURT DIPPING SAUCE:

¼ cup (60 g) mayonnaise

¼ cup (60 g) plain yogurt

1 teaspoon lemon juice

1 tablespoon (4 g) minced fresh dill, plus a pinch for sprinkling

1 teaspoon minced garlic

YOU WILL ALSO NEED:

Toothpicks

1. Bring a large pot of water to a boil.

2. Slice the artichoke in half lengthwise. Carefully place in the boiling water and boil for 30 minutes, or until you can easily pull away one of the lower leaves. Remove artichoke halves and set aside. Place the asparagus stalks in the pot and boil for 2 minutes.

3. Remove the stalks from the cooked artichoke halves. Press 4 broccoli stems into each flat half of the artichokes (for legs).

4. Cut the asparagus spear to the desired length (for a tail) and press into the large end of the artichoke.

5. Cut the chicken or turkey slice into 2 triangles for heads. Place a toothpick on one side of the slice and push into the artichoke to fix the head in place.

6. Mix the mayonnaise, yogurt, lemon juice, dill, and garlic in a small bowl. Place in a small dish and sprinkle dill on top.

7. To eat, pull off the artichoke petals and dip the bases into the dill-yogurt sauce. Pull the bases through your teeth to remove the pulp from the end of the petal. Spoon out the fuzzy center and throw away. Dip the artichoke heart into the sauce and eat.

Bean appétit!

Makes 2 Armadill-Yos

note

Use this dill-yogurt dip to make Supergyros on page 38.

DO-RE-FOR-ME

This musical munchie was named the National Restaurant Association's Best Kids' Meal in the United States!

2 slices whole wheat bread

1½ tablespoons (24 g) nut, seed, or soy butter

1 tablespoon (20 g) natural strawberry jam

1 slice pumpernickel bread

1. Use a knife to remove crusts from bread and cut into a large rectangle shape.

2. Spread nut, seed, or soy butter across one slice of bread. Spread jam across the other slice of bread. Stack the slices of bread. Cut sandwich into fourths and place side-by-side to make keys.

3. Cut pumpernickel bread slice into three little rectangles to make the "black keys," and place each on a crack at the top of the wheat bread, between the "white keys."

Bean appétit!

Makes 1 Do-Re-for-Me

bean there, ate that

Try a new tune with these additional combos:

• Nut, seed, or soy butter + Apricot jam + Pomegranate seeds

• Nut, seed, or soy butter + Honey + Granola + Dried fruit

• Nut, seed, or soy butter + Apple butter + Freeze-dried apple slices

note

If your child isn't a fan of pumpernickel bread, use the dark side of the crusts for the black keys instead.

LOLLIPAWS

Your family will paw over these hot little pockets.

1 cup (140 g) diced cooked chicken

¼ cup (65 g) pesto

1 container biscuit dough

2 pieces of string cheese, cut into 48 thin rounds

4 slices of provolone or mozzarella cheese

YOU WILL ALSO NEED:

12 lollipop sticks

Child scissors

Small circle cookie cutter (optional)

1. Preheat oven to 350°F (180°C).

2. In a small bowl, combine the cooked chicken and pesto.

3. Carefully peel each biscuit into 4 thinner layers. Place half of them 4 inches (10 cm) apart on greased baking sheets.

4. Place a lollipop stick in the middle of each biscuit round so it almost reaches the other side (see opposite, bottom). Use a spoon to put 1 tablespoon (9 g) of chicken mixture in the center of each biscuit layer. Place 1 thin circle of string cheese on top.

5. Top each round with a biscuit layer. Pinch at the sides to prevent filling from spilling out. Make sure to especially pinch around the lollipop stick so it stays secure. Bake for 11 minutes or until golden brown.

6. Use a small round cookie cutter or child scissors to cut 12 circles from the provolone or mozzarella cheese slices. The circles should be slightly larger than the string cheese circles.

7. Immediately after taking pockets out of the oven, flip them over so the flat sides face up. Gently press 3 string cheese circles at the top of the circle and 1 provolone cheese circle at the bottom center of the circle to form a paw shape.

8. Place back in the oven for 2 minutes for the cheese to adhere to the biscuit. Let cool slightly and then eat.

Bean appétit!

Makes 10 to 12 Lollipaws

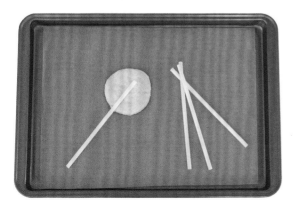

bean there, ate that

Try filling the pocket with scrambled eggs, veggies, and cheese for breakfast Lollipaws.

MASH OF THE PENGUINS

This potato-meatball mash-up is the coolest.

1 cup (256 g) black beans, rinsed and drained

1 pound (455 g) lean ground turkey breast

1 egg white, beaten

1 teaspoon onion powder

½ teaspoon garlic powder

½ teaspoon salt

½ cup (55 g) Italian breadcrumbs

20 carrot circles, about ⅛ inch (3 mm) thick

1 cup (225 g) mashed potatoes, heated

YOU WILL ALSO NEED:

Child scissors

Toothpicks

note

You can freeze extra meatballs and use later to make Spagiggles (recipe page 41).

1. Preheat the oven to 400°F (200°C).

2. Mash black beans in a large mixing bowl. Mix in ground turkey, egg white, onion powder, garlic powder, and salt. Fold in breadcrumbs.

3. Use ⅔ of the mixture to form into 2-inch (5-cm) balls. Place on a baking tray lined with foil. Use your fingers to press the meatballs into flat oval shapes, about ½ inch (1.3 cm) thick.

4. Use the other ⅓ of the mixture to form 1-inch (2.5-cm) meatballs and place on the foil-lined tray. Cook all meatballs for 20 minutes or until they are no longer pink in the center.

5. While the meatballs are cooking, use the scissors to cut each carrot circle into a triangle foot. Snip 2 mini triangles from the wide end of the triangles to create toes. Save snippings for the penguins' beaks.

6. Once cooked, slice a thin strip off the thin end of one of the oval meatballs so it can stand easier. Save the meatball crumbs.

7. Place a toothpick in one of the round meatballs (the head), and push the toothpick down the long side of the oval meatball to form a complete body.

8. Use a spoon or a toothpick to spread the mashed potatoes on the meatball body to make a white belly and face. Place the carrot nose on the face with 2 of the meatball crumbs for eyes. Stand upright with the triangle feet sticking out of the body.

Bean appétit!

Makes 10 to 12 penguins

TASTE BUDS

Two halves make a whole friendship with this wrap.

¼ cup (60 g) Greek yogurt

¾ teaspoons curry powder

Pinch of salt

½ teaspoon Dijon mustard

¼ teaspoon lemon juice

½ teaspoon honey

½ teaspoon extra-virgin olive oil

1 cup (150 g) diced Granny Smith apples

1 cup (140 g) cooked chicken breast, diced

2 tablespoons (20 g) diced red onion (optional)

1 cup (30 g) baby spinach leaves

3 pieces flatbread

6 olive slices

3 zucchini rounds, cut in halves

1. In a mixing bowl, combine first 7 ingredients (yogurt through extra-virgin olive oil) and whisk until combined.

2. Add the apples, chicken, and red onion (optional) to the mixture and toss to coat.

3. Scatter spinach on the top and bottom of each flatbread, making sure some of the spinach hangs over the edges. Top with the chicken mixture.

4. Roll flatbread from side to side so the spinach pokes out both edges. Lightly press down after rolling to make sure the sandwich doesn't unwrap.

5. Cut each wrap in halves. Add 2 olive slices on each half as eyes and 1 zucchini half as a mouth.

Bean appétit!

Makes 3 sets of Taste Buds (6 buddies altogether)

bean there, ate that

What other veggies can you experiment with to create the faces and hair?

note

If you have a cake pop maker, feel free to use that instead when baking the falafel balls—it will make the falafel more circular. Pour ⅛ teaspoon extra-virgin olive oil in the wells and bake falafel mixture for 10 minutes.

note

Save the asparagus stalks to make Armadill-Yo on page 19. And use the liquid from the can of chickpeas to create the Meringue Gang dessert on page 129.

A-SPARE-AGUS

Your family will be bowled over by these falafel balls.

¼ cup (40 g) diced onion

¼ cup (15 g) parsley

¼ cup (15 g) cilantro

1½ teaspoons minced garlic

1 teaspoon ground cumin

¼ teaspoon salt

¼ teaspoon baking soda

1 tablespoon (8 g) flour

1 egg

1 15-ounce (425 g) can garbanzo beans, drained

1 tablespoon (15 ml) extra-virgin olive oil

10 asparagus stalks

½ cup (113 g) hummus plus extra for dipping falafel

YOU WILL ALSO NEED:

Small ice cream scooper (optional)

Pastry brush (optional)

1. Preheat oven to 400°F (200°C).

2. Place the first nine ingredients (onion through egg) in a food processor and pulse until coarsely chopped. Blend in garbanzo beans. Let the mixture stand for 10 to 15 minutes.

3. Use a small ice cream scooper or spoon to scoop 1 tablespoon (14 g) of mixture and place on a baking sheet lined with parchment paper. Use a pastry brush or your finger to lightly coat the falafel balls with extra-virgin olive oil.

4. Bake for 15 to 18 minutes. The falafel will spread out a bit. Once cooked, and while they are still warm, use your fingers to form the falafel balls into a more perfect circle.

5. While the falafel balls are baking, fill a small pot with 2 cups (475 ml) of water and bring to a boil. Also prepare a small bowl with 2 cups (475 ml) ice water.

6. Cut the asparagus tips off in 1 to 1½-inch (2.5 to 3.7 cm) segments. If you have skinny asparagus cut them shorter so they can more easily stand. Place in the boiling water for 2 to 3 minutes until they turn bright green. Immediately remove them and place in the ice water to stop the cooking.

7. Dab the cut ends of the asparagus tips with hummus and stand up in a triangle shape on a plate. Take turns "bowling" with the falafel balls before you dig in.

Bean appétit!

Makes 16 to 18 bowling balls

WHOOPSIE DAISY

You won't be able to leaf this foodie flower alone.

1 can (5 oz or 142 g) tuna, drained

2 tablespoons (28 g) mayonnaise

2 teaspoons (10 g) plain Greek yogurt

1 red bell pepper

1 zucchini cut into 10 round slices

2 celery stalks

1 cherry tomato cut in half

4 spinach leaves

1. Mix the tuna, mayonnaise, and yogurt. Set aside.

2. Cut the red bell pepper widthwise into two ½-inch (1.3-cm) rings. Remove the seeds and core. Set the rest of the pepper aside for dipping.

3. Place 5 zucchini rounds on each plate. Top with a red bell pepper ring. Spoon the tuna salad into the pepper rings. Top with a cherry tomato half.

4. Place a celery stalk at the base of the red pepper rings for a stem. Add spinach leaves to the stems.

Bean appétit!

Makes 2 Whoopsie Daisies

note

Chicken salad also works well inside the red pepper ring.

ITSY BITSY BITER

Celery and olives make this sandwich
a silly sort of spider bite.

2 slices whole wheat bread

1 teaspoon mustard (optional)

2 slices deli turkey

5 slices pepperoni

1 teaspoon balsamic
   vinaigrette (optional)

¼ cup (30 g) shredded
   mozzarella cheese

Cooking spray

4 celery sticks

2 olive slices

YOU WILL ALSO NEED:

Large circle cookie cutter
   (optional)

1. Cut the slices of bread with a circle cookie cutter or rim of a drinking glass.

2. Spread mustard (optional) on one slice and top with turkey and pepperoni. Drizzle balsamic vinaigrette (optional). Sprinkle mozzarella cheese and top with other slice of bread.

3. Grill sandwich in pan coated with cooking spray over medium heat. Once lightly browned, flip the sandwich over and continue grilling until cheese is melted.

4. Cut the celery sticks in halves lengthwise. Place the 8 celery pieces around the sandwich for legs. Top the sandwich with 2 olive slices for eyes.

Bean appétit!

Makes 1 Itsy Bitsy Biter

GNOCCHi POKEY

There's no right or wrong design here—poke the gnocchi to construct anything you can imagine.

1 medium beet, roasted
  and peeled

1 egg

1 cup (250 g) ricotta cheese

¼ teaspoon salt

2 cups (250 g) flour

2 tablespoons (28 g)
  unsalted butter

Your favorite sauce for dipping

YOU WILL ALSO NEED:

Toothpicks

1. Place the beet, egg, ricotta cheese, and salt in a food processor and blend until smooth.

2. Place mixture in a medium bowl and add half the flour. Stir. Add the rest of the flour and stir. Use your hands to briefly knead the dough until everything is combined (you don't want to overwork it, or the gnocchi turns out tough). Cover with plastic wrap and let sit for 30 minutes.

3. Divide dough into four sections. On a lightly floured surface, use your hands to roll the first section of dough into a ½-inch-thick (1.3 cm) rope. Cut the rope into 1-inch (2.5 cm) segments. If desired, lightly press the tines of a fork on the segments to create lines. Repeat with rest of the dough.

4. Fill a large pot with water and bring to a boil. Boil the gnocchi in batches, for about 3 minutes, until they float.

5. Melt the butter in a large pan over medium heat. Place cooked gnocchi in the pan and lightly brown on either side, about 1 to 2 minutes per side.

6. Pierce and combine gnocchi with toothpicks to create any three-dimensional design you'd like. Serve with your favorite sauce—a creamy white sauce is especially delicious.

Bean appétit!

Serves 8

bean there, ate that

Rice paper has a neutral flavor and works
with both savory and sweet ingredients.
Try making a Snack-a-Pillar stuffed with
fruit salad and a strawberry head.

SNACK-A-PiLLAR

See-through rice paper makes assembling this sandwich transformational.

FOR THE FILLING:

2 tablespoons (30 ml)
rice vinegar

2 tablespoons (30 ml)
low-sodium soy sauce

1 tablespoon (16 g) nut,
seed, or soy butter

½ teaspoon sesame oil

½ teaspoon minced garlic

1 cup (225 g) shredded
rotisserie chicken

½ cup (38 g) chopped
snow peas

1 cup (55 g) chopped romaine
lettuce

¼ cup (45 g) diced mango

½ cup (65 g) carrot matchsticks

**TO ASSEMBLE THE
SNACK-A-PILLAR:**

4 pieces of circular rice paper

1 cup (40 g) pretzel sticks

8 raisins

4 roma tomatoes

8 carrot matchsticks

YOU WILL ALSO NEED:

Toothpicks

To make the filling:

1. Whisk the rice vinegar, soy sauce, nut butter, sesame oil, and garlic in a large mixing bowl until smooth. Add the chicken, snow peas, lettuce, mango, and carrot matchsticks and toss.

To make the Snack-a-Pillar:

1. Fill a large flat bowl or pan with warm water and place one piece of rice paper into the bowl. Let the rice paper soak until it is soft, about 1 minute. Carefully place it on a clean, flat surface.

2. Spoon ½ cup (112 g) of the mixture across the center of each circle, leaving space on each side.

3. Fold the outer two sides in and roll up the paper as if you're making a burrito or a log. Place on plate and carefully slice the roll into five slices.

4. Place pretzel sticks around the body for legs. Cut a ½-inch (1.3 cm) slice from the flat end of the tomato. Place it at one end of the caterpillar. Balance the other side of the tomato on top to make a goofy grin.

5. Use a toothpick to poke eye holes in the tomato and press in the raisins. Poke two more holes on top of the head and push in carrot matchsticks.

6. Repeat with other sheets of rice paper.

Bean appétit!

Makes 4 Snack-a-Pillars

SUPERGYRO

You don't need superhero powers to make this sandwich disappear.

1 tablespoon (15 ml) extra-virgin olive oil

1 cup (140 g) cooked diced chicken breast

1 teaspoon minced garlic

1 teaspoon dried oregano

4 pita rounds

2 tablespoons (30 g) dill-yogurt sauce from Armadill-Yo recipe, page 19, divided

1 cucumber, cut into round slices

1 spinach tortilla

YOU WILL ALSO NEED:

Child scissors

To make the filling:

1. Heat the extra-virgin olive oil in a large skillet over medium-low heat. Add the chicken, garlic, and oregano and stir until heated through, about 3 to 5 minutes.

To assemble the pita:

1. Use the child scissors to cut each pita round into a large triangle (like a pizza slice), about 4 to 5 inches (10 to 13 cm) long. Spread 1 teaspoon (5 g) of the dill-yogurt sauce inside each triangle.

2. Carefully lay 3 cucumber slices flat on top of the yogurt in each pita and gently fill with the chicken mixture.

3. Use the scissors to cut the tortilla into whatever shape you'd like to create your family's Supergyro logo. Use the remaining dill-yogurt sauce to glue the tortilla logo shapes into place on the outside of the pita.

Bean appétit!

Makes 4 Supergyros

behind the beans

One of the best-selling grown-up sandwiches on our menu is a cross between a super hero and a magician: The Great Turkado.

SPAGIGGLES

Unleash your inner stylist with these sassy bites.

¼ cup (35 g) cooked spaghetti

2 teaspoons (10 ml)
   extra-virgin olive oil

¼ teaspoon garlic powder

¼ teaspoon salt

12 turkey-black bean
   meatballs, warmed (from
   Mash of the Penguins,
   page 25)

Marinara sauce or your favorite
   pasta sauce for dipping

YOU WILL ALSO NEED:

Child scissors (optional)

1. Preheat the oven to 400°F (200°C).

2. Toss the cooked spaghetti with the olive oil, garlic powder, and salt until evenly coated.

3. Use child scissors or your fingers to pinch off the spaghetti strands into different lengths. Place the noodles on a foil-lined baking sheet in whatever hairstyles you like—curlicues, spikes, etc. Bake for 5 to 6 minutes or until lightly browned.

4. Let cool slightly. Fix the spaghetti hair onto the meatballs and serve with your favorite pasta sauce for dipping.

Bean appétit!

Makes 12 stylin' meatballs

bean there, ate that

Try using the noodles to create
stick figures for your Spagiggles.

THE SKEW LAGOON

Teriyaki chicken skewers are the center of this taste of the tropics.

FOR THE TREE TRUNKS:

2 teaspoons (10 ml) lime juice

1 teaspoon honey

¼ teaspoon garlic powder

2 boneless skinless chicken
    breasts

1 tablespoon (15 ml)
    extra-virgin olive oil

1 tablespoon (15 ml)
    teriyaki sauce, divided

**FOR THE REST OF THE TREES
AND ISLANDS:**

2 tablespoons (30 g)
    cream cheese

1 pineapple, cut into four
    1 inch- (2.5 cm) thick round
    slices with peel removed

2 cups (60 g) baby spinach
    leaves

8 freeze-dried blueberries
    (optional)

YOU WILL ALSO NEED:

Skewers

To make the tree trunks:

1. Mix the lime juice, honey, and garlic powder in a medium bowl.

2. Slice each chicken breast into 4 long strips. Place in the bowl with the lime juice mixture and coat all pieces evenly.

3. Heat the extra-virgin olive oil in a large skillet over medium heat. Place the chicken on the skillet and cook for 3 minutes on each side.

4. Drizzle 2 teaspoons (10 ml) of the teriyaki sauce over the chicken. Toss the chicken in the sauce so that all sides are coated. Cook for one more minute or until the center is no longer pink. Remove from heat and set aside.

To make the rest of the trees and islands:

1. In a small bowl, mix the cream cheese and the remaining teaspoon of teriyaki sauce.

2. Push a skewer lengthwise into each chicken slice. Stick two chicken skewers onto each pineapple slice for the tree trunk.

3. Use the cream cheese mixture as glue to stick the spinach leaves onto the top of the skewers.

4. If desired, place freeze-dried blueberries on the pineapple for coconuts.

Bean appétit!

Makes 4 Skew Lagoons

bean there, ate that

If you want to crank up the crunch on your tropical island, try sprinkling the pineapple slices with brown sugar and cinnamon and baking for 10 to 12 minutes at 350°F (180°C).

behind the beans

At Bean Sprouts, playfulness is one our core values. Sometimes you can catch us hula dancing with spinach leaves when we're making these tropical trees.

MAC AND CHEETAH

This mushroomy mac and cheese will hit the spots!

1 cup (225 g) cottage cheese

1 package (8 oz or 225 g)
baby bella mushrooms (or
about 20 small baby bella
mushrooms)

1 teaspoon extra-virgin olive oil

1 cup (235 ml) milk, divided

1 tablespoon (8 g) flour

½ cup (40 g) shredded
Parmesan cheese

2 cups (225 g) shredded
cheddar cheese, divided

½ teaspoon salt

6 cups (840 g) cooked
macaroni, about 2½ cups
(263 g) dry pasta

1. Preheat oven to 350°F (180°C).

2. Puree the cottage cheese in a food processor. Set aside.

3. Carefully remove the stems from the mushrooms. Slice the mushroom caps into thin rounds (see opposite, bottom). You should be able to get about two rounds that have a hole in the center from each mushroom. Finely dice the stems and non-hole rounds.

4. Heat the extra-virgin olive oil in a large pan over medium heat. Cook all the mushroom rounds and the diced mushrooms for 4 to 5 minutes. Carefully flip over the circles and gently stir the diced mushrooms. Cook for another 4 to 5 minutes. Let cool slightly. Gently separate the rounds from the diced mushrooms and and set aside.

5. Whisk ¼ cup (60 ml) milk and flour in a medium saucepan before putting it on the stovetop. Heat over medium, whisking constantly for about 1 to 2 minutes. Slowly pour in the remainder of the milk, continuing to whisk until the sauce thickens, about 1 to 2 more minutes.

6. Remove saucepan from heat. Stir in the cooked diced mushrooms, pureed cottage cheese, Parmesan cheese, 1 cup (112 g) cheddar cheese, and salt.

7. Gently toss with macaroni and pour into a shallow 2-quart baking dish. Sprinkle the remaining 1 cup (112 g) cheddar cheese. Top with the mushroom circles.

8. Cover dish with foil and bake for 15 minutes. Remove foil and broil for 3 minutes until cheese is melted, but not browned.

Bean appétit!

Serves 6 to 8

bean there, ate that

Not a fan of mushrooms? Try olive slices instead.

GRILLEDZILLA

Make sure the ends of googly-eyed Grilledzilla's mouth are pointing up in a slight smile, so he doesn't scare anyone away.

Cooking spray

2 slices wheat bread

2 slices cheddar cheese

¼ cup (30 g) shredded mozzarella cheese

2 zucchini rounds

2 olive slices

1. Preheat skillet over medium heat.

2. Spray cooking spray on one slice of bread. Flip over and layer one slice of cheddar, shredded mozzarella, and the other slice of cheddar cheese. Top with other slice of bread and spray the top slice of bread with cooking spray.

3. Grill sandwich in pan until lightly browned and flip over; continue grilling until cheese is melted.

4. Cut a zigzag line through the bottom third of the sandwich. Place zucchini rounds at the top of the sandwich and top with olives for eyes.

Bean appétit!

Makes 1 Grilledzilla

bean there, ate that

Give your Grilledzilla some zip with these additional combos:

• Turkey + Mayonnaise + Cheddar cheese + Apple slices

• Grilled chicken slices + BBQ sauce + Gruyere cheese

BEAN FRIENDS FOREVER

Inspired by the best friends forever necklaces we used to wear as kids, we stuffed these heart pockets with a three-bean chili.

FOR THE FILLING:

1 cup (160 g) diced onion

2 garlic cloves, minced

1 pound (455 g) ground turkey

1 tablespoon (7.5 g) chili powder

1 teaspoon dried oregano

1 teaspoon ground cumin

½ teaspoon salt

1 can (14.5 ounce or 411 g) diced tomatoes, undrained

1 can (15.5 ounce or 439 g) red kidney beans, undrained

½ cup (128 g) canned black beans, undrained

½ cup (128 g) canned navy beans (also called Great Northern Beans), undrained

FOR THE HEART POCKET:

1 store-bought piecrust

Flour for dusting work surface

1 egg, beaten

YOU WILL ALSO NEED:

Pastry brush (optional)

To make the filling:

1. In a large pan, cook the onion, garlic, and ground turkey over medium heat for 8 to 10 minutes until the meat is no longer pink. Drain the liquid and return to the stovetop.

2. Add the rest of the ingredients for the filling. Do not to drain the tomatoes or beans; simply add the liquids to the pan. Bring to a boil over high heat.

3. Reduce heat to medium low, until the mixture is gently bubbling. Cook uncovered for about 20 minutes or until desired thickness. Let cool slightly.

To make Bean Friends Forever heart pockets:

1. Preheat the oven to 350°F (180°C).

2. Roll the dough on a floured surface as thin as possible. Use a knife to cut 4 to 6 identical heart shapes, about 6 inches (15 cm) tall.

3. On half of the crusts, place one line of chili along each side, leaving about ½-inch (1 cm) margins (see opposite, lower left). Top with another crust. Press down the middle of each heart so the dough sticks together.

4. Use a knife to cut a zigzag down the middle of the hearts (see opposite, lower right). Separate the halves. Pinch the sides of the dough, sealing the edges. Use a pastry brush to lightly coat the tops with the beaten egg.

5. Place on baking sheet lined with parchment paper and bake for 15 to 18 minutes or until lightly browned.

Bean appétit!

Makes 2 to 3 sets of Bean Friends Forever hearts, plus leftovers

WRAP STAR

I'm a wrap star, yo
A veg burrito
Just greens, no meat
Now drop that beat!

14 ounces (397 g) firm tofu,
    drained and patted dry

1 tablespoon (7.5 g) packaged
    taco seasoning

1 tablespoon (15 ml)
    extra-virgin olive oil

1 to 2 red cabbage leaves

8 Bibb lettuce leaves,
    washed and patted dry

1 avocado cut into 8 slices

1 cup (70 g) broccoli slaw
    or coleslaw

½ cup (70 g) bean sprouts

½ cup (130 g) salsa (optional)

YOU WILL ALSO NEED:
Child scissors

1. Cut the tofu into 8 slices lengthwise. Generously sprinkle both sides of the slices with taco seasoning.

2. Heat the extra-virgin olive oil in a large pan over medium high. Place the tofu slices in the pan and cook for about 5 minutes on each side until crispy.

3. Use the child scissors to cut 8 sunglasses shapes from the red cabbage leaves. If there is extra cabbage, add accessories or scenery.

4. Fill each lettuce leaf with a crispy tofu slice. Add avocado, slaw, sprouts, and salsa, if desired. Fold the sides of the lettuce wrap over the center. Press hard so the lettuce snaps into place and does not unfold. Flip over and place the sunglasses on the leaf.

Bean appétit!

Makes 8 Wrap Stars, yo

NiBBLES

Snack time is an easy stunt with Daredeviled Eggs and other bold bites.

CROCAMOLE

This croc pot is delightful for dipping veggies.

1 avocado, sliced in half lengthwise

½ cup (113 g) hummus

1 teaspoon lemon juice

4 zucchini rounds, plus more for dipping

4 olive slices

14 matchstick carrots

Other favorite veggies for dipping, such as baby carrots or celery sticks

1. Use a spoon to scoop out the avocado pulp and place in a bowl. Set avocado skins aside.

2. Add the hummus and lemon juice to the bowl and use a fork to mash ingredients until smooth.

3. Scoop the green hummus back into the avocado skins. Place 2 zucchini rounds and olive slices in the hummus at the wider end of each avocado skin for eyes. Add carrot matchsticks at the narrow end for teeth.

4. Enjoy with your favorite veggie dippers.

Bean appétit!

Makes 2 Crocamoles

behind the beans

We almost named this dish "Guacadile." Creating clever names is a favorite part of our jobs.

FRUIT 66

Get your kicks with this fruit dip mix!

½ cup (125 g) whole milk
  ricotta cheese

1 teaspoon honey

Pinch of cinnamon

Assorted fruits

YOU WILL ALSO NEED:

Child scissors

1. In a small bowl, stir the ricotta cheese, honey, and cinnamon.

2. Using the backside of a spoon, scoop the ricotta and smear a line of it onto a plate to create the road.

3. Use child scissors to snip little pieces of fruit (we used grapes) and place in the center of the ricotta road for the center dividing line.

4. Experiment with different fruits to create automobiles, using the ricotta mixture as glue. Place the fruit cars along the ricotta road.

Bean appétit!

Makes enough dip for 3 to 4 cars

bean there, ate that

Try using different fruits to construct these vehicles:

- Semi-truck
- Convertible
- Station wagon
- School bus
- Racecar
- Limousine

XYLOFUN

Try multicolored carrots to make this dish really ring.

Cooking spray

8 carrots

1½ teaspoons (7 g) unsalted butter, melted

1 tablespoon (15 ml) pure maple syrup

⅛ teaspoon salt

12 capers

2 pitted olives (optional)

Cooking spray

YOU WILL ALSO NEED:

Pastry brush (optional)

Lollipop sticks (optional)

Child scissors

1. Preheat oven to 425°F (220°C). Line a baking sheet with aluminum foil and spray with cooking spray.

2. Peel the carrots. Carefully slice in halves lengthwise.

3. Mix the butter and maple syrup in a small bowl. Use a pastry brush or the back of a spoon to brush the mixture on both sides of the carrots. Place the carrots rounded side down on the baking sheet. Sprinkle with salt. Bake for 20 minutes or until fork tender.

4. Place the two largest carrot halves, rounded side down, turned inwards at a slight angle, like you're making a "greater than" math sign. Balance remaining carrots flat side up across the two large, angled carrots.

5. Trim the ends of the carrots with the scissors so they don't extend beyond the bottom carrots. Place a caper on the end of each carrot key.

6. If desired, place an olive on the end of each lollipop stick for mallets.

Bean appétit!

Makes 2 Xylofuns

behind the beans

We strike up our own percussion section at Bean Sprouts café when it's a customer's birthday. Our Bean Team shouts to the crowd, "Can I get a drumroll, PEAS?" After everyone drumrolls, we all yell "YipPEA!" to the birthday child.

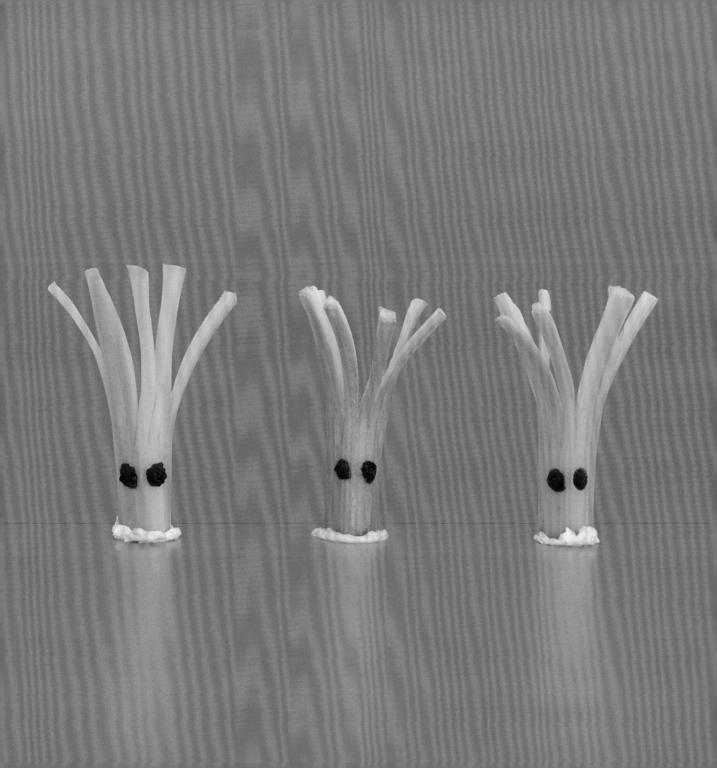

TROLL PATROL

Celery-brate this quirky nod to Ants on a Log.

½ cup (115 g) cottage cheese

2 tablespoons (32 g) creamy nut, seed, or soy butter

2 teaspoons (13 g) honey

10 to 12 celery sticks (about half a bunch)

¼ cup (35 g) raisins

1. Blend cottage cheese, butter, and honey in a food processor until smooth.

2. To create the hair, cut the celery sticks into thin slices, leaving 1½ inches (3.8 cm) intact at one end.

3. Fill the intact part of each celery stick with the butter mixture. Dip 2 raisins in the mixture and fix onto the front side for eyes.

4. Lightly coat the bottom of the celery sticks with the mixture and use as glue to balance upright.

Bean appétit!

Makes 10 to 12 trolls

bean there, ate that

Soaking the cut celery sticks in ice water for a few minutes will make the "hair" branch out and look even sillier!

UFOats

This twist on energy balls is out of this world.

¼ cup (65 g) nut, seed, or soy butter

¼ cup (56 g) mashed sweet potato

2 tablespoons (40 g) honey

¼ teaspoon pumpkin pie spice

½ cup (78 g) old-fashioned oats

2 tablespoons (22 g) mini chocolate chips

10 dried pineapple rings

YOU WILL ALSO NEED:

Child scissors

1. In a large bowl, blend the nut butter, sweet potato, honey, and pumpkin pie spice. Add the oats and stir until evenly distributed.

2. Use your hands and roll little chunks of the mixture into 1-inch (2.5 cm) balls. Place 6 to 8 mini chocolate chips around the top of the ball for UFO portholes. Place on plate and chill for 30 minutes.

3. Use child scissors to enlarge the center hole of the pineapple rings so they fit onto the center of the sweet potato balls.

Bean appétit!

Makes 8 to 10 UFOats

UNDER THE Z

This silly use of zucchini noodles brings the "z" to under the sea.

Cooking spray

2 cups (240 g) spiral zucchini noodles plus 16 to 20 zucchini noodles

½ cup (40 g) shredded Parmesan cheese

1 egg

¼ cup (31 g) flour

YOU WILL ALSO NEED:

Round waffle maker

1. Preheat the waffle maker. Lightly coat the iron with cooking spray.

2. In a bowl, blend the 2 cups (240 g) spiral zucchini noodles, Parmesan cheese, egg, and flour. Pour into the waffle maker and spread evenly across the surface so the mixture reaches the edges of the iron.

3. While the waffle is cooking, place the remaining zucchini noodles on the bottom halves of two plates.

4. Remove the waffle and cut in half. Place each waffle half at the top of the noodles to create the jellyfish.

Bean appétit!

Makes 2 jellyfish

note

You can use store-bought zucchini noodles or make your own if you have a spiralizer. Or cut zucchini into long, thin noodle-like strips (a mandoline works great for this).

BUG BITES

These crunchy critters offer a fun take on pepper poppers.

½ cup (93 g) cooked quinoa, cooled

2 tablespoons (9 g) diced broccoli, raw or cooked

2 tablespoons (16 g) diced carrots, raw or cooked

1 tablespoon (14 g) ranch dressing

12 sweet baby bell peppers

2 celery stalks

1. Stir the quinoa, broccoli, carrots, and ranch dressing in a bowl. Set aside.

2. Cut the tops off the sweet baby bell peppers and set aside. Use your fingers to pinch out the seeds and thin core.

3. Cut the celery stalk into 48 segments, about ¼ inch (6 mm) thick.

4. Use your fingers or a spoon to fill the baby bell peppers with the quinoa mix. Lay flat on a plate or plates. Press the tops back on the peppers and arrange 4 celery segments around the peppers for legs.

Bean appétit!

Makes 12 Bug Bites

note

Bug Bites can be filled with any veggies you like. If you prefer a good crunch, keep the veggies raw.

HIPPEA DIPPEA

Give peas a chance with these cheesy chips.

FOR THE DIP:

1½ cups (225 g) peas

¾ cup (195 g) ricotta cheese

½ cup (40 g) shredded
   Parmesan cheese

1 teaspoon minced garlic

¼ teaspoon salt

½ cup (15 g) spinach leaves

FOR THE PEACE SIGNS:

1 cup (80 g) shredded
   Parmesan cheese

1. Preheat the oven to 400°F (200°C).

2. Place all of the dip ingredients in a food processor. Pulse until desired consistency (we like ours lumpy, but make yours smoother if you prefer). Set aside.

3. Line a large baking sheet with parchment paper. To make each peace sign, pour 2 teaspoons (4 g) of Parmesan cheese on parchment paper. Use your fingers to pinch it into a ring, about 3 inches (7.5 cm) in diameter.

4. Use 1 teaspoon more of Parmesan cheese to create the inside lines of the peace sign. Make sure the cheese is bunched up enough so they're not too thin when cooked.

5. Keep making peace signs according to steps 3 and 4 until you've used all the Parmesan cheese.

6. Bake for 4 to 5 minutes or until golden and crisp. Cool.

7. Dip the groovy signs in the Hippea Dippea.

Bean appétit!

Serves 3 to 4

note

We've found the cooking time of the Parmesan peace sign crisps varies, based on the brand of cheese. Keep a close eye on the oven so it doesn't overcook.

behind the beans

At Bean Sprouts we say, "Peas out" anytime we sign off emails, end a presentation, etc.

PEARACHUTE

An upside down cupcake liner elevates the presentation of these ginger pear mini muffins.

1 cup (125 g) flour

½ cup (115 g) brown sugar plus 1 tablespoon (15 g) brown sugar, divided

¾ teaspoon baking powder

½ teaspoon salt

1 tablespoon (7 g) ground flax meal

¼ teaspoon ground ginger

¼ teaspoon cinnamon

1 egg

½ teaspoon pure vanilla extract

¼ cup (60 g) unsweetened applesauce

2 tablespoons (30 ml) extra-virgin olive oil

¼ cup (46 g) cooked quinoa

1 cup (150 g) finely diced Bartlett pear (about 1 medium pear)

YOU WILL ALSO NEED:

Mini muffin pan

20 mini cupcake liners

20 pieces of dried angel hair pasta

20 large cupcake liners (for decoration)

1. Preheat oven to 350°F (180°C).

2. In a large mixing bowl, blend the flour, ½ cup (115 g) brown sugar, baking powder, salt, flax meal, ground ginger, and cinnamon.

3. In a small bowl, mix the egg, vanilla extract, applesauce, and extra-virgin olive oil. Stir in the quinoa.

4. Stir the wet ingredients into the dry ingredients until blended. Do not overmix. Fold in the diced pear.

5. Spoon the batter into a mini muffin pan lined with mini cupcake liners.

6. Sprinkle the 1 tablespoon (15 g) brown sugar evenly over the tops. Bake for 10 to 12 minutes. Let cool.

7. Break the angel hair pasta into halves. Press 2 strands around the edges of the mini muffins and balance a large cupcake liner upside down on top.

Bean appétit!

Makes 20 Pearachutes

VEGETA-BLAZE

This is a recipe kids can pretty much do all by themselves and one of the only times they get to play with fire.

1 slice cheddar cheese

4 to 6 baby carrots, cut in half lengthwise

¼ cup (56 g) hummus

4 to 6 pretzel sticks, broken in pieces

8 to 10 grapes (all one color or different colors)

YOU WILL ALSO NEED:

Child scissors

1. Use child scissors to cut the cheese into flame shapes. Cut the ends of the baby carrot slices into points, like flames.

2. Spread hummus on a plate in a circle about 2 to 3 inches (5 to 7.5 cm) in diameter.

3. Press the bottom of the carrot and cheese flames into the hummus to build your campfire. Place the pretzel pieces in small piles close to the flames for logs.

4. Use the child scissors or a table knife to cut each grape in half lengthwise. Place each half flat-side down around the campfire.

Bean appétit!

Makes 1 Vegeta-Blaze

note

If you want a red-hot fire, cut red bell peppers into flame shapes and add them to the blaze.

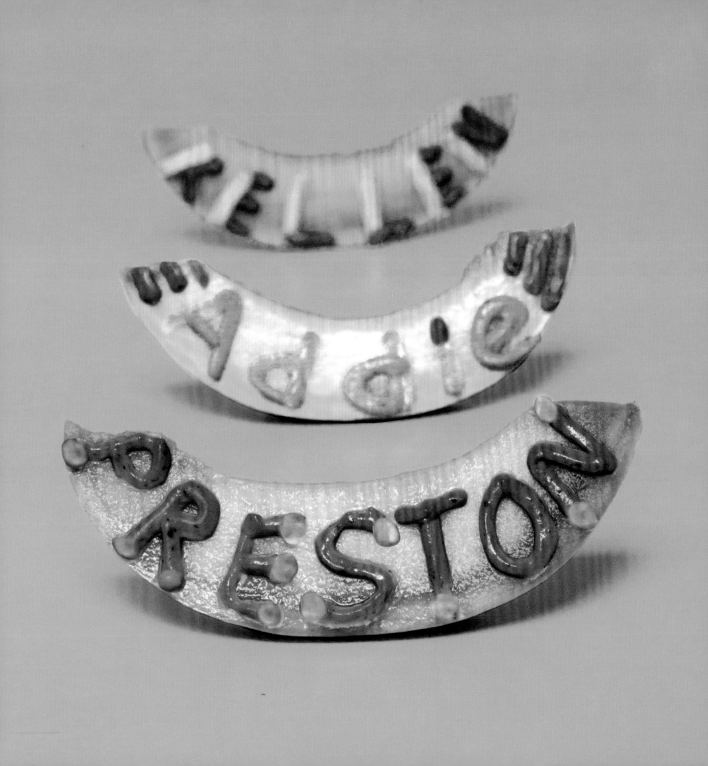

HONEY DOODLE

Inspired by the amazing hands-on art exhibits at children's museums, we use honeydew melon slices as our canvases for place cards.

½ honeydew melon,
  cut into slices

8-ounce package (226 g)
  cream cheese, divided

1 cup (145 g) blueberries

¼ teaspoon ground ginger

1 banana

⅛ teaspoon cinnamon

½ cup (75 g) strawberries

3 mint leaves

¼ teaspoon honey

YOU WILL ALSO NEED:

Piping bags or resealable
  sandwich bags

1. Use a food processor to blend each of the combinations below to make different Honey Doodle colors.

2. Scoop each mixture into its own bag. Decorate the honeydew slices with doodle letters to make mealtime place cards for your friends and family.

Combo 1:

Blueberries + Ground ginger + ⅓ package cream cheese

Combo 2:

Strawberries + Mint leaves + ⅓ package cream cheese + Honey

Combo 3:

Banana + Cinnamon + ⅓ package cream cheese

Bean appétit!

Makes 10 to 12 Honey Doodle slices

bean there, ate that

Try using a squeeze bottle to aid in decorating—it is inexpensive and can add pizzazz to any plate. Create a marinara maze, or a game of tzatziki tic-tac-toe. Edible doodles make mealtime much more adventurous!

EENIE, MEENIE, MINEY

This silly snack is a great way to use leftover veggies and dips from other recipes in this book. You don't have a to waste a thing.

2 tablespoons each:
- Crocamole filling (28 g; page 55)
- Whoopsie Daisy tuna salad (26 g; page 30)
- Armadill-Yo dill-yogurt dip (30 g; page 19)

18 round crackers

3 hardboiled eggs, sliced into rounds

A variety of vegetables (carrot matchsticks, broccoli florets, zucchini, etc.)

1. Use a spoon to spread the dips on the round crackers. Top with a hardboiled egg slice.

2. Use little pieces of vegetables to create funny faces.

Bean appétit!

Makes 18 cracker faces

bean there, ate that

For a sweeter snack, substitute kiwi slices for the eggs, fruit for the veggies, and the Fruit 66 ricotta dip (page 56) and the Troll Patrol mixture (page 60) in place of the savory spreads.

FLUTTER BITES

Nutritional yeast's cheesy flavor helps these oversized tortilla chips take flight.

1 tablespoon (4 g)
   nutritional yeast

½ teaspoon onion powder

½ teaspoon garlic powder

¼ teaspoon salt

6 red pepper tortillas

1 tablespoon (15 ml)
   extra-virgin olive oil

18 grape tomatoes

6 marinated small fresh
   mozzarella balls

YOU WILL ALSO NEED:

Child scissors

Pastry brush (optional)

Aluminum foil

Toothpicks

1. Preheat oven to 450°F (230°C).

2. Mix the nutritional yeast, onion and garlic powders, and salt in a small bowl. Set aside.

3. Lightly fold a tortilla in half (making sure not to break the tortilla at the fold). Using child scissors, cut a butterfly wing shape using the fold as the center (see opposite, lower left). Cut a design in the wing. Unfold to see the whole butterfly. Repeat with remaining tortillas.

4. Use the pastry brush to brush each side of the wings with extra-virgin olive oil. Sprinkle both sides with the dry mixture.

5. Roll aluminum foil into six 1-inch-thick (2.5 cm) log shapes, about the length of your butterflies. Place the logs on a baking sheet and balance tortilla fold on top to create a slight bend in the wings (see opposite, lower right). Bake for 4 to 6 minutes, until lightly brown and toasted.

6. Use toothpicks to connect 3 grape tomatoes for a body, plus 1 mozzarella ball for a head. Cut a thin slice off of the bottom tomato so the kabob can stand up. Repeat until you have 6 kabobs.

7. Place the kabobs upright (for the butterfly bodies) and balance the tortilla chip wings around the tomatoes.

Bean appétit!

Makes 6 Flutter Bites

note

Save scraps of tortillas for the Supergyro recipe on page 38.

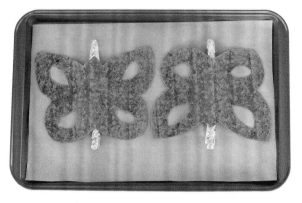

BROCTOPUS

This colorful creature is inspired by the baked vegetable tots we serve with every kids' meal at Bean Sprouts.

2 cups (142 g) steamed broccoli florets

¼ cup (40 g) diced white or yellow onion

2 tablespoons (8 g) chopped parsley

½ teaspoon salt

1 egg

⅔ cup (33 g) panko breadcrumbs

⅓ cup (38 g) shredded cheddar cheese

1 tablespoon (15 ml) extra-virgin olive oil

YOU WILL ALSO NEED:

Parchment paper

Pastry brush (optional)

1. Preheat the oven to 400°F (200°C).

2. Add broccoli, onion, and parsley to a food processor and pulse until coarsely chopped. Add salt, egg, panko breadrumbs, and cheese to the food processor and pulse until incorporated.

3. Use your hands to roll 1½ tablespoons (17 g) of mixture into a tot shape. Place on a large baking sheet lined with parchment paper. Repeat three times for a total of four tots.

4. Use the rest of the mixture to create 4 sets of 8 Broctopus legs (32 legs total) on the parchment paper. Form skinny legs and pinch to create curves.

5. Use the pastry brush or your finger to brush extra-virgin olive oil on the tops of all the pieces. Bake for 15 to 18 minutes, without flipping the pieces over.

6. Place the tot upright and surround with 8 legs. Dip the sea creature into ranch dressing or ketchup or enjoy plain.

Bean appétit!

Makes 4 Broctopi

CHIPWRECK

Experience a wave of flavor with these roasted veggies.

1 medium eggplant

½ cup (80 g) diced onion

1 medium sweet potato

¼ teaspoon dried basil

¼ teaspoon garlic powder

¼ teaspoon salt

1 tablespoon (15 ml)
extra-virgin olive oil

2 big handfuls of blue
corn tortilla chips

YOU WILL ALSO NEED:

Child scissors

Toothpick

*bean there,
ate that*

Add dabs of Greek yogurt
or sour cream to the blue chip
"waves" for whitecaps.

1. Slice the eggplant diagonally, lengthwise (see opposite, lower left). Cut a thin slice off the longer side of the eggplant so it can stand up at an angle (see opposite, lower right). Use a spoon to hollow out a pocket in the long cut side.

2. Use a blade of the child scissors to notch little portholes in the side of the eggplant. Balance the eggplant on a platter with the hollowed part facing up.

3. Dice the eggplant that you cut off and scooped. Place In a bowl. Add diced onion.

4. Cut the sweet potato in half lengthwise. Dice one half and add to the bowl with other diced vegetables. Set the other half of the sweet potato aside.

5. Toss the diced vegetables with the basil, garlic powder, and salt. Heat extra-virgin olive oil in a large pan over medium heat. Add the diced vegetables. Cook for 15 minutes, stirring occasionally, until lightly browned and fork-tender.

6. Use a peeler or child scissors to remove a stripe of skin near the top of the sweet potato half. Place a toothpick in the other end of the sweet potato, and push into the scooped out part of the eggplant for the ship stack.

7. Scatter the blue corn tortilla chips around the eggplant. When the vegetables are done, use them to fill the hollowed part of the eggplant. Spill the extra veggies onto the deck, spilling down onto the chips.

Bean appétit!

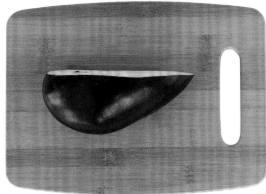 

DAREDEVILED EGGS

If only all deviled eggs had the moxie of these go-getters!

3 large kale leaves

1 tablespoon (15 ml) extra-virgin olive oil

¼ teaspoon salt

6 hard-boiled eggs, peeled

¼ cup (60 g) mayonnaise

1 teaspoon Dijon mustard

12 thin red bell pepper slices, about ½ inch long (13 mm)

YOU WILL ALSO NEED:

Child scissors

Toothpick

note

Try serving the Daredeviled Eggs on top of tall, clear cups turned upside down, so it looks like they're flying.

1. Preheat oven to 375°F (190°C).

2. Use the child scissors to cut one of the kale leaves until you have ⅓ cup (22 g) little confetti-like pieces. Set aside.

3. With the other large kale leaves, cut 6 triangle shapes for capes, about 3 to 4 inches (7.5 cm to 10 cm) long. Use your fingers or a pastry brush to coat both sides of the capes with olive oil. Place on foil-lined baking sheet and sprinkle with sea salt. Bake for 8 to 10 minutes or until toasted.

4. Cut a tiny slice off the bottoms of the wide ends of each egg so they can stand up. Cut off the top third of each egg and carefully remove the yolks and place in a small bowl.

5. Add the mayonnaise, Dijon mustard, and kale confetti and stir until blended. Carefully spoon the egg yolk mixture back into the hollowed-out eggs.

6. Use a toothpick to poke 2 small holes in the top of each egg white and push in 2 red pepper pieces for horns.

7. Carefully press the short end of each baked kale cape onto the top of the egg yolk mixture so that it's "flying" straight out. Top with the smaller piece of the hard-boiled egg.

Bean appétit!

Makes 6 Daredeviled Eggs

SiPS

Mr. Purple Gurple and pals bring you
creative ways to think inside the cup!

SiP-A-DEE-DOO-DAH

This pretty petal lemonade will make you pucker.

2 lemons

2 cups (290 g) whole
   strawberries, plus
   4 whole strawberries

¼ cup (85 g) honey

3 cups (709 ml) cold water

YOU WILL ALSO NEED:

Child scissors or grapefruit
   spoon

Sieve

Small flower cookie cutter
   (optional)

2 straws, cut in half

note

This sipper is tastiest when
you chill the strawberries and
lemons before making.

1. Carefully cut off the top third of each lemon widthwise.

2. Holding the lemons above a blender, use a spoon to scoop out the insides. Put all of the insides—the juice, pulp, and even the seeds—in the blender.

3. Use child scissors or grapefruit spoon to cut out the segment walls as best you can from the inside of the lemon halves. Cut a small slice off the pointy end of the lemon halves so they can stand on their own. Set aside.

4. Add 2 cups (290 g) whole strawberries, honey, and water to the blender and blend until smooth.

5. Pour mixture through a sieve and into a container. Chill in the refrigerator while you finish the rest of the steps.

6. Use a table knife or child scissors to cut the greens from the top of the 4 whole strawberries. Move the knife or scissors ½ inch (1.3 cm) down each strawberry and cut a round slice.

7. Use the cookie cutter (or child scissors) to cut flower shapes from the strawberry rounds. Carefully wedge a flower on the end of each straw.

8. Pour the lemonade into each lemon cup and gently push a straw down into the bottom of each lemon rind to stand the flowers straight up.

Bean appétit!

Makes 2 lemon cups plus lots of refills

MR. PURPLE GURPLE

A mustache gives this beverage a pop of personality and panache.

1 natural fruit leather roll

1 cup (155 g) frozen blueberries

¼ cup (62 g) frozen raspberries

⅓ cup (77 g) vanilla yogurt

¼ cup (60 ml) grape juice

¼ cup (60 ml) water

YOU WILL ALSO NEED:

Child scissors

1. Use the child scissors to snip a 2-inch (5 cm) section of the fruit roll. Fold the fruit roll in half with the paper on the inside.

2. Cut half a mustache shape. Carefully open the halves back up and remove the paper backing to reveal a whole mustache. Stick the mustache on the side of the cup.

3. Blend all ingredients in a blender until smooth. Pour into the glass.

Bean appétit!

Makes 1 Mr. Purple Gurple

bean there, ate that

Take your trimmings one step further and cut out fruit leather eyebrows or beards.

EXPERi-MINT

If you don't have beakers lying around, try test tubes from your child's science kit or any skinny glass to show off that mad scientist mojo.

1 cup (235 ml) milk
  (of your choice)

1 frozen banana

¼ ripe avocado

½ cup (15 g) spinach leaves

8 mint leaves

1 tablespoon (11 g)
  chocolate chips

YOU WILL ALSO NEED:

4 beakers (optional)

1. Blend all ingredients in a blender until smooth. Pour into your beakers or skinny glasses.

Bean appétit!

Makes 4 Experi-MINTs

behind the beans

We like to shake things up when it comes to cooking with kids. In the past, we've used (clean) Frisbees for plates, plastic baseball bats for rolling pins, and Legos for cookie cutters.

FINTASTIC FLOATIES

Floating fruit fish add a friendly topper to this berry oat smoothie.

1 cup (250 g) frozen sliced nectarines or peaches

1 cup (155 g) frozen blueberries

¼ cup (40 g) old-fashioned oats

½ cup (115 g) vanilla yogurt

1 cup (235 ml) milk (of your choice)

4 thawed nectarine slices

10 thawed blueberries

YOU WILL ALSO NEED:

Mini fish cookie cutter (optional)

1. Place the frozen sliced nectarines or peaches and frozen blueberries in a blender with the oats, yogurt, and milk. Blend until smooth.

2. Pour smoothie in 2 wide-rimmed cups. Using the mini fish cookie cutter, cut 4 fish from the thawed nectarine slices. Top each smoothie with 2 fish and add thawed blueberries for bubbles.

Bean appétit!

Makes 2 smoothies

behind the beans

At Bean Sprouts cafés, we make this same design on our Under the Sea-Za veggie pizzas. We use zucchini and red peppers for the fish shapes and olive slices for bubbles.

CLEMENTINY BUBBLES

This bitty beverage brings you bubbly bliss.

18 to 20 kumquats

2 clementines

½ cup (120 ml) naturally
flavored lime seltzer water

YOU WILL ALSO NEED:

Strainer

1. Cut off the top third of the kumquats and place in a food processor. Use the handle of a spoon to hollow out the top of each kumquat, creating a little hole. Set aside.

2. Use a knife to score a line around the top third of the clementine peels. Peel off the top third and discard the peel.

3. Use your thumb to loosen the peel from the clementine segments. Carefully remove the segments so that the peel stays in one piece. Place the segments in a food processor and puree with the kumquat tops.

4. Over a small bowl, strain the puree using a strainer, capturing the juice. Discard the pulp.

5. Add the lime seltzer water. Carefully pour the juice into the clementine peels and tiny kumquat cups. Refill them as many times as you'd like. Then eat the kumquats with the juice all in one bite, peel and all!

Bean appétit!

Serves 2 with refills

bean there, ate that

What other tiny fruits can you try in place of kumquats?
Try raspberries or hollowed out strawberries. Just be
sure to hold them in your hands while pouring,
in case they can't stand up on their own.

PINK PATOOTIE

Embrace your inner Peacasso—try your own imaginative spin with the cupcake liners and see what else you can create.

1 cup (255 g) frozen strawberries

½ fresh banana

⅓ cup (77 g) vanilla yogurt

½ cup (120 ml) pineapple juice

½ cup (120 ml) water

YOU WILL ALSO NEED:

Child scissors

2 colorful cupcake liners

Scotch tape

1. Blend all ingredients in a blender until smooth. Pour into a glass.

2. Use the child scissors to cut out the circle base of each cupcake liner. Cut a line along a ridge of the liners so they each unroll into one long piece.

3. Wrap one cupcake liner around the glass. Use Scotch tape on the edges of the liner to fasten. Wrap the next liner so that a little bit of the first liner is showing and tape together.

Bean appétit!

Makes 1 Pink Patootie

behind the beans

A grumpy grandpa once came into Bean Sprouts, mad at the world. He tried to order a Pink Patootie and couldn't stop giggling as he said the silly name. It turned his day around!

TIRAMI-SHOE

You'll fall head over heels for this tiramisu-inspired hot cocoa.

2 cups (475 ml) milk
(of your choice)

2 tablespoons (15 g)
cocoa powder

2 tablespoons (25 g)
cane sugar

2 tablespoons (15 g)
vanilla protein powder

2 tablespoons (30 g)
mascarpone cheese

2 large all-natural
marshmallows

YOU WILL ALSO NEED:

Child scissors

Rolling pin

1. Heat milk in a small pot, removing from heat before it starts to boil. Add the cocoa powder, sugar, protein powder, and mascarpone cheese, and gently stir with a whisk until smooth.

2. Use the child scissors to cut each marshmallow in half lengthwise. Use the rolling pin to roll and flatten the marshmallow halves. Cut the flattened marshmallows into shoe shapes.

3. Divide the Tirami-Shoe cocoa into 2 mugs and top each with a pair of marshmallow shoes.

Bean appétit!

Makes 2 Tirami-Shoe cocoas

SiP HOP

This carroty concoction will put a spring in your step.

1 cup (130 g) chopped carrots

2 teaspoons (10 ml) pure
    maple syrup

½ cup (85 g) frozen
    pineapple chunks

¼ teaspoon cinnamon

Pinch of nutmeg

1 cup (235 ml) canned
    coconut milk

1 whole carrot, for garnish

1 tablespoon (15 g) cream
    cheese, divided

1 tablespoon (5 g)
    unsweetened shredded
    coconut, divided

1. Place the chopped carrots, maple syrup, pineapple, cinnamon, nutmeg, and coconut milk in a blender and blend until smooth. Pour into a cup or glass.

2. Cut the whole carrot in half lengthwise. Trim into rounded segments about 3 to 4 inches long (7.5 to 10 cm) for bunny ears.

3. Press 1 teaspoon of cream cheese in a smaller segment on the flat side of one of the carrot ears. Gently press 1 teaspoon shredded coconut on the cream cheese. Repeat. Place the bunny ears in the top of the smoothie.

4. Form a little ball with the remaining teaspoon cream cheese. Roll in the rest of the shredded coconut to form a bunny tail. Press on the other side of the cup.

Bean appétit!

Makes 1 Sip Hop

BREAKFAST BITES

From breakfast branches to edible ogres,
turn your mornings into *mmm*-ornings!

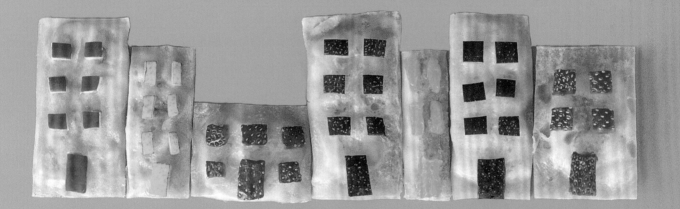

SKYCRÊPER STICKS

A mash-up of crêpes and French toast sticks builds the foundation of this breakfast.

¼ cup (63 g) ricotta mixture from Fruit 66 recipe (page 57)

¼ cup (58 g) nut, seed, or soy butter mixture from Troll Patrol recipe (page 61)

12 square or rectangle wonton wrappers

1 egg, beaten

Cooking spray

½ cup (90 g) your favorite diced fruits

Syrup, for dipping (optional)

1. Dab 2 teaspoons of either the ricotta or butter mixture on one half of a wonton wrapper, leaving a little space at the edge. Lightly dab the edge of the wrapper with water. Fold the empty side of the wrapper over and press the edges to seal.

2. Gently place the sealed wrappers in a bowl with the beaten egg. Flip over so all sides are coated.

3. Cook in a skillet coated with cooking spray for 3 minutes. Turn over and cook for another 1 to 2 minutes until lightly browned.

4. Place rectangular wontons in a line to resemble a skyscraper. Use the diced fruits to decorate the pieces with windows and doors. Dip in syrup, if desired.

Bean appétit!

Makes 12 Skycrêper Sticks

bean there, ate that

Cut the wonton wrappers into different shapes to create different sized buildings.

OGRE PARFAIT

Keep calm and ogre on—these dry-erase markers wipe off easily.

½ cup (50 g) granola, divided

2 firm green pears, divided
(Green Anjou pears
work well)

2 kiwi, peeled

1 cup (230 g) vanilla yogurt

YOU WILL ALSO NEED:

Dry-erase markers

1. Divide the granola between 2 glasses.

2. Cut 1 pear into slices, and place in a food processor, along with the kiwi and yogurt. Blend until smooth. Spoon on top of granola.

3. Cut the other pear into fourths and cut into ogre ear shapes. Carefully cut a thin notch into the bottom of each pear ear, about ½ inch (1.3 cm). Press the notch onto the glass rims for ears.

4. Use the dry-erase markers to draw funny ogre faces on the front of the glasses.

Bean appétit!

Makes 2 Ogre Parfaits

BUMBLE BEANS

You'll bee abuzz over this yummy breakfast.

FOR THE BUMBLE BEANS:

Cooking spray

6 eggs

¼ cup (60 ml) water

¼ teaspoon salt

½ cup (128 g) black beans, rinsed and drained

12 mini waffles, toasted

FOR THE FLOWERS:

1 cup (170 g) diced strawberries

½ cup (65 g) diced raspberries

¼ cup (40 g) diced pineapple

¼ cup (45 g) diced mango

6 whole raspberries

YOU WILL ALSO NEED:

Child scissors

Oval cookie cutter (optional)

1. Preheat oven to 400°F (200°C).

2. Spray an 8 x 8-inch (20 x 20 cm) pan. Place eggs, water, and salt in the pan and use a fork or whisk to scramble. Bake in oven for 10 minutes. Set aside to cool briefly.

3. Meanwhile, combine the diced fruit in a bowl. Set aside.

4. When the eggs are slightly cool, use the cookie cutter or a table knife to cut an oval shape, about 3 to 4 inches (7.5 to 10 cm) and place each near the edge of a plate.

5. Lay 3 stripes of black beans on the eggs. Place one mini waffle on either side for wings.

6. Use a spoon to place ⅓ cup (52 g) of diced fruit on the other edge of the plate. Arrange in a flower shape. Top with a whole raspberry in the center. Repeat.

Bean appétit!

Makes 6 servings

behind the beans

Shannon's first Bean Name was "Queen Bean," but she soon realized it sounded too bossy. So she switched her Bean Name to "Peacasso" because she loved bringing her creativity to Bean Sprouts.

FRO-BO

This frozen bowl is our riff on a breakfast ice pop and is packed with berried treasure.

¾ cup (175 ml) milk
(of your choice)

¾ cup (28 g) your
favorite cereal

3 strawberries, cut into slices

YOU WILL ALSO NEED:

Cereal bowl and a bowl
slightly smaller than
your cereal bowl

Duct tape (optional)

1. Fill cereal bowl with 1 inch (2.5 cm) milk. Sprinkle some cereal in the bottom of the bowl.

2. Place the small bowl in the center of the cereal bowl. Add remaining milk, remaining cereal, and strawberry slices into the gap between the bowls.

3. If the smaller bowl keeps floating up, either duct tape the rim to the rim of the cereal bowl so they remain at the same height, or add some ice cubes to the inside of the small bowl to keep it in place. Make sure the small bowl is not touching the bottom of the cereal bowl—you want to leave about 1 inch (2.5 cm) at the bottom. Freeze overnight or until solid.

4. When you're ready to eat your frozen breakfast bowl, remove the bowls from the freezer and let sit for about 10 minutes until both the cereal bowl and smaller bowl are easy to separate. Place just the frozen bowl on a plate to catch any drips.

Bean appétit!

Makes 1 Fro-Bo

bean there, ate that

Fill your Fro-Bo with your favorite
fruit salad, a yogurt parfait,
or any other breakfast food
that tastes yummy
when chilled!

bean there, ate that

Try making the buds using thinly-sliced eggplant or green zucchini to add colors to your bouquet.

POSH BLOSSOMS

A breakfast bouquet to start your day in a lovely way.

6 ciabatta rolls or other hard rolls

2 yellow squash

1 tablespoon (15 ml) extra-virgin olive oil

¼ cup (25 g) shredded Parmesan cheese

1 teaspoon dried basil

1 teaspoon salt

6 eggs

YOU WILL ALSO NEED:

Mandoline (optional)

Pastry brush (optional)

1. Preheat the oven to 350°F (180°C).

2. Cut a 2-inch (5 cm) circle in the top crust of each roll. Use your fingers to remove the circular piece of crust and most of the inside of the roll, but leave the bottom crust intact. Place rolls on a foil-lined baking sheet. Set aside.

3. Use a mandoline or knife to cut 12 extremely thin slices of squash. Place on flat surface. Use pastry brush or spoon to lightly coat both sides of each slice with extra-virgin olive oil.

4. Evenly sprinkle the Parmesan cheese, basil, and salt on the sides facing up. Set aside.

5. In a small cup, beat the eggs. Evenly pour the eggs in the holes of the rolls.

6. Place 2 squash slices in one long line, with the ends overlapping slightly. Start at one end and tightly roll the slices (see opposite, bottom). Wedge in the hole of the roll. Repeat for the other slices.

7. Bake for 45 minutes to 1 hour, or until the eggs are firm. Serve warm.

Bean appétit!

Makes 6 Posh Blossoms

HOOTABAGA

A flighty feast of turkey sausage and rutabaga hash browns is owl right.

FOR THE OWL:

1 teaspoon dried sage

1 teaspoon salt

¼ teaspoon ground black pepper

⅛ teaspoon dried marjoram

1 pound (455 g) ground turkey

1 piece string cheese cut into 16 small circles

1 slice cheddar cheese

YOU WILL ALSO NEED:

Child scissors (optional)

FOR THE TREE:

2 cups (220 g) grated rutabaga (about 1 medium rutabaga)

½ cup (80 g) diced onion

¼ cup (31 g) flour

1 egg

½ teaspoon garlic powder

½ teaspoon salt

2 tablespoons (30 ml) extra-virgin olive oil

Handful of spinach leaves

To make the owl:

1. Mix sage, salt, black pepper, and marjoram together in a large bowl. Add ground turkey and stir until incorporated.

2. Use a ¼-cup (56 g) scoop to divide the ground turkey into 8 equal amounts. On a tray lined with parchment paper, form the portions into long oval patties.

3. At one end of the oval, pinch two triangles for ears. Pinch in the sides of the oval to create a head and body (see opposite, bottom). Freeze the tray for 10 minutes so the owls more easily hold their shape.

4. Coat a large skillet with cooking spray and place over medium heat.

5. Cook the patties for 3 minutes and flip. Cook another 3 minutes until the center is no longer pink.

6. Place the string cheese circles near the pointy ears for owl eyes.

7. Use the child scissors to cut small circles and small triangles from the cheddar cheese slice and place for pupils and a beak.

To make the tree:

1. Blend the rutabaga, onion, flour, egg, garlic powder, and salt in a bowl.

2. Heat extra-virgin olive oil in a large skillet over medium-high heat. Add mixture. Cook for 5 minutes, flip, and cook 5 minutes more until crispy.

3. Remove from heat and use a knife to cut into strips. Place in tree shape with owl sausages on the branches. Add spinach leaves for greenery.

Bean appétit!

Serves 4 to 6

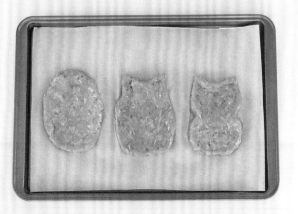

behind the beans

Unlike owls, we are not at all nocturnal—sometimes we start our Bean Sprouts creative meetings as early as 5 a.m. That's the time we're the most imaginative.

DJ CRISP

Pancake puff earphones bring the beats to this baked apple with a cinnamon crisp topping.

½ cup (78 g) old-fashioned oats

1 teaspoon cinnamon

¼ cup (60 g) packed brown sugar

2 tablespoons (14 g) ground flax meal

2 tablespoons (28 g) unsalted butter, melted

4 large tart apples

4 pieces natural licorice

8 pancake puffs, warmed (see recipe note)

YOU WILL ALSO NEED:

Apple corer (optional)

Toothpicks

1. Preheat oven to 375°F (190°C).

2. In a small bowl, combine the oats, cinnamon, brown sugar, flax meal, and butter. Set aside.

3. Use an apple corer or spoon to core the apples, but make sure to leave the base intact so the filling doesn't spill out. Pack the mixture into the apples.

4. Arrange apples in a baking dish so they don't touch. Add ¾ cup (175 ml) water to the dish, or enough to cover the bottom. Bake for 45 to 50 minutes until the apples are soft.

5. Use a toothpick to secure the licorice in a headband shape. Add a pancake puff to each toothpick for the earmuffs.

Bean appétit!

Makes 4 apples

note

If you can't find pancake puffs in your grocery store freezer section, use regular mini pancakes or mini muffin tops.

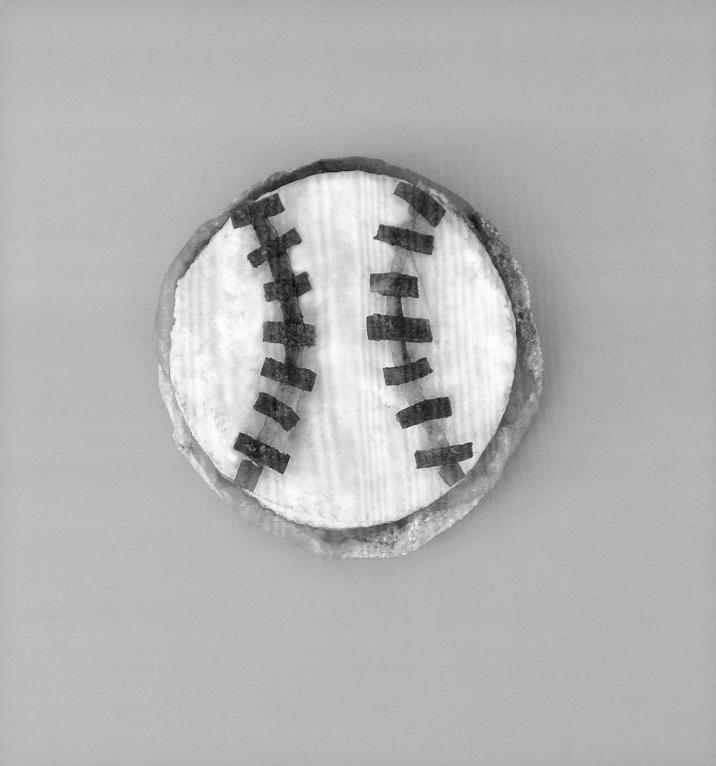

BREAK FASTBALL

This sporty start to the morning is sure to be a hit.

1 slice uncooked turkey bacon

4 egg whites

⅛ teaspoon sea salt

Cooking spray

1 English muffin, toasted

2 slices of your favorite cheese

YOU WILL ALSO NEED:

Child scissors

Mason jar lid ring
   (center removed)

1. Use the child scissors to cut the uncooked turkey bacon into 4 3-inch (7.5 cm) slightly curved thin strips. Cut the rest of the turkey bacon into 30 or so ½-inch (1.3 cm) thin strips. Cook to desired crispiness. Set aside.

2. Scramble the egg whites and salt.

3. Spray a small nonstick pan and the inside of the mason jar lid with cooking spray. Place the circle on the pan with the flat side down and heat to medium.

4. Pour half of the scrambled egg whites in the ring. Pour 2 tablespoons (30 ml) water around the circle and cover. Steam the egg until it's cooked all the way through, about 3 to 4 minutes. Repeat, making sure to spray the ring with cooking spray again.

5. Top each toasted English muffin half with a cheese slice and then an egg circle.

6. Place the longer curved turkey bacon strips on the egg first, then balance the little strips on the longer line to resemble a baseball.

Bean appétit!

Makes 2 Break Fastballs

behind the beans

Some of our favorite baseball Bean Names are "Jackie Robeanson," "The Great Bambeano," and "Joe DiMaggiokra."

TREATS

Travel through time—from dinos to pea-mojis.
You'll dig these desserts packed with personality!

GREEN GOBBLER

The kiwi to a kid's heart is this scrumptious sorbet.

6 kiwis, cut in half widthwise

1 tablespoon (15 ml) lime juice

2 tablespoons (40 g) honey

6 green grapes, cut in half
    widthwise

12 mini chocolate chips

Mint sprigs (optional)

YOU WILL ALSO NEED:

3 straws

1. Cut a little slice off the fuzzy end of each kiwi half, so that the half can easily stand up.

2. Use a spoon to scoop out the insides of the kiwi and place in food processor. Save 6 of the skins.

3. Add the lime juice and honey to the food processor and blend until smooth. Place in a flat dish and put in the freezer until solid, about 2 hours.

4. After the mixture is frozen, cut each straw into 4 pieces and place half of a green grape on each straw piece. Place a mini chocolate chip, point side first, in the middle of each grape.

5. Scoop the frozen kiwi sorbet into the kiwi skin. Fix the straws with eyes into the kiwi and add a mint sprig to give it eclectic eyebrows.

Bean appétit!

Makes 6 Green Gobblers

Wi-Pie

These protein-packed pies send a strong signal it's dessert time.

1¼ cups (219 g) mini semi-sweet milk chocolate chips, divided

¼ cup (60 ml) milk (of your choice)

14 ounces (397 g) firm tofu, drained and patted dry

1 tablespoon (15 ml) pure vanilla extract

5 frozen waffles, thawed

1 banana, cut into 20 slices

YOU WILL ALSO NEED:

Regular-size muffin tin

To make the filling:

1. Melt 1 cup (175 g) chocolate chips in a small bowl in the microwave for 30 seconds at a time, stirring in between. Place melted chocolate, milk, tofu, and vanilla extract in a food processor and blend until extremely smooth. Chill for at least 1 hour.

To make the Wi-Pies:

1. Preheat the oven to 375°F (190°C).

2. Press the thawed waffles into a muffin tin to form cups. Bake for 12 to 15 minutes or until lightly browned. Remove from tins and let cool completely.

3. Place 3 to 4 banana slices in the bottom of each waffle crust. Top with ½ cup (115 g) chocolate pudding, or until it reaches the rim of the waffle cup. Place the remaining mini chocolate chips on top in 4 arched lines to resemble a wi-fi icon.

Bean appétit!

Makes 5 Wi-Pies

note

Take the full time to chill the pudding—this helps ease the tofu taste and brings out the chocolate flavor.

THE MERINGUE GANG

"Aquafaba" is the name for the liquid left over from soaking or cooking legumes, or in this case, the liquid found in a can of chickpeas. It's important that you chill the aquafaba before using it in this recipe.

¼ cup (60 ml) aquafaba, chilled

¼ cup (50 g) plus 1 tablespoon (13 g) superfine sugar

Natural food coloring

4 dozen small strawberries

10 to 12 seedless grapes

YOU WILL ALSO NEED:

Hand or stand mixer

Resealable sandwich bag

Child scissors

bean there, ate that

There are several ways to cook with aquafaba—from making your own mayonnaise to baking it in brownies.

1. Preheat the oven to 200°F (93°C).

2. In a medium glass bowl, use a hand mixer or stand mixer to whip the aquafaba until stiff peaks form (in other words, if you held the bowl upside down, nothing would fall out), about 6 to 7 minutes. Slowly add the sugar a little bit at a time, whipping after each addition.

3. Place 3 to 4 drops of natural food coloring in a resealable sandwich bag and press the bag flat so the drops spread across the entire bag. Carefully spoon the aquafaba mixture into the bag.

4. Cut a small hole in the corner of the bag and squeeze quarter-size circles onto a parchment-lined baking tray. Bake for 75 minutes. Turn the oven off, and open the oven door slightly. Leave the tray in the oven for another 45 minutes so they can dry out.

5. Use child scissors to cut the greens off the tops of the strawberries. Also cut the points off, so the strawberries can stand on their own.

6. Cut the grapes into slices widthwise and cut each slice in half. Place 2 grape halves near each tip of the strawberries for feet. Top each strawberry with a meringue hat.

Bean appétit!

Makes 48 meringues

PEA-MOJi COOKiES

A sweet treat to show someone how you really feel.

FOR THE COOKIES:

1½ teaspoons (7 ml) pure vanilla extract

1 stick (112 g) unsalted butter, softened

⅓ cup (80 g) canned chickpeas, rinsed and drained

¾ cup (170 g) packed light brown sugar

¼ teaspoon salt

1½ cups (188 g) flour

1 tablespoon (7 g) ground flax meal

¼ teaspoon baking powder

FOR THE FROSTING:

½ cup (115 g) cream cheese

¼ cup (30 g) powdered sugar

½ teaspoon pure vanilla extract

1 tablespoon (15 g) plain Greek yogurt

Natural food coloring

YOU WILL ALSO NEED:

Resealable sandwich or piping bag

Circle cookie cutter (optional)

To make the cookies:

1. Preheat oven to 350°F (180°C).

2. Add vanilla extract, butter, and chickpeas to a food processor and blend until smooth and fluffy. Add brown sugar and blend.

3. In a large bowl, blend salt, flour, flax meal, and baking powder. Add the butter mixture and stir just until combined.

4. Wrap in plastic wrap and chill in refrigerator, for about 30 minutes or until dough has hardened.

5. Roll dough on a lightly floured surface to ¼-inch (6 mm) thick. Use a circle cookie cutter or the rim of a glass to cut circle shapes.

6. Place on a greased baking sheet and bake for 10 to 12 minutes. Let cool completely.

To make the frosting:

1. Mix the cream cheese, powdered sugar, vanilla extract, and Greek yogurt with a hand blender on high speed, about 2 to 3 minutes.

2. Spoon 2 tablespoons of the frosting in a small bowl and add 2 to 3 drops each red and blue food coloring to create a dark color. Put frosting in a piping or plastic sandwich bag and snip off the corner.

3. In the remaining bowl of frosting add 4 to 6 drops green food coloring. Frost the entire surface of the cookies with the green frosting. Use the darker frosting to pipe whatever Pea-Moji design you'd like.

Bean appétit!

Makes 10 Pea-Moji cookies

behind the beans

We are incredibly enthusiastic about our clean guidelines. Even our frosting and sprinkles at Bean Sprouts are made with natural food coloring.

POP'S CORN

Dress up plain popcorn with this suit-worthy snack.

6 cups (64 g) air-popped popcorn, divided

2 tablespoons (30 g) tahini, divided

¼ cup (80 g) blueberry preserves

¼ cup (80 g) raspberry preserves

YOU WILL ALSO NEED:

Child scissors

Parchment paper

1. Use the child scissors to cut a piece of parchment paper into two tie shapes. Set aside.

2. Divide popcorn into two large bowls.

3. Heat 1 tablespoon (15 g) tahini and blueberry preserves in a small bowl in the microwave for 45 seconds, until bubbly. Pour over one bowl of popcorn and gently stir until all popcorn is coated.

4. Repeat Step 3 with the remaining 1 tablespoon (15 g) tahini, raspberry preserves, and the second bowl of popcorn.

5. Work quickly to press the popcorn on the parchment paper shapes to create your personally-designed ties. Let cool before eating.

Bean appétit!

Makes 2 ties

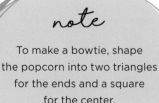

note

To make a bowtie, shape the popcorn into two triangles for the ends and a square for the center.

behind the beans

We don't wear fancy ties at Bean Sprouts. The back of our T-shirts read "Don't worry, bean happy!"

DINO S'MORES

We've found chocolate to be a much friendlier tar pit for our prehistoric pals.

¾ cup (94 g) whole wheat flour

½ cup (63 g) all-purpose flour

¼ cup (28 g) ground flax meal

½ teaspoon baking powder

¼ teaspoon baking soda

¼ cup (56 g) butter, softened

¼ cup (60 g) packed
  brown sugar

3 tablespoons (60 g) honey

½ teaspoon pure vanilla
  extract

¼ cup (60 ml) milk
  (of your choice)

1 cup (175 g) chocolate chips

2 green pears

YOU WILL ALSO NEED:

Waxed paper

Rolling pin

Dinosaur cookie cutters

Child scissors

1. Preheat oven to 350°F (180°C). Mix the flours, flax meal, baking powder, and baking soda into a bowl.

2. In a separate bowl, use a hand mixer to blend the butter, brown sugar, honey, and vanilla extract until fluffy, about 2 minutes.

3. Stir the butter mixture into the flour mixture. Add milk. Stir until blended.

4. Place dough on a piece of waxed paper. Flatten into a big circle and place in the freezer for 15 minutes.

5. On a floured surface, roll the dough to about ¼-inch (6 mm) thick. Press the dinosaur cookie cutters in the dough. Place shapes on an ungreased cookie sheet. Bake for 8 to 10 minutes. Let cool.

6. Melt the chocolate chips in a small bowl in the microwave for 30 seconds at a time, stirring in between. Spoon 2 tablespoons (28 g) of melted chocolate on a small piece of waxed paper and quickly place a dinosaur upright in each chocolate glob.

7. Place the dinosaurs and chocolate in the freezer, until the chocolate hardens, about 2 to 3 minutes. Carefully peel off the chocolate tar pits from the waxed paper and stand dinosaurs upright on a plate.

8. Cut pears into slices, and cut slices into tree shapes for the background. Use the pear slices in place of marshmallows for fruit-filled s'mores.

Bean appétit!

Makes 10 to 12 Dino S'mores

PUDDING GREENS AND DONUT HOLES-IN-ONE

These golf goodies are par for the dessert course.

FOR THE PUDDING GREENS:

1 cup (235 ml) coconut milk

¼ cup (8 g) spinach leaves

2 tablespoons (30 ml) pure
maple syrup

¼ cup (36 g) chia seeds

To make the Pudding Greens:

1. Place the coconut milk, spinach leaves, and the maple syrup in a food processor and blend until smooth. Transfer to a medium bowl.

2. Stir in the chia seeds. Let sit for 15 minutes, stirring occasionally. Refrigerate the mixture for an hour or until set.

3. Divide the pudding between 4 shallow dishes.

Makes "fore" (4) Pudding Greens

(continued)

bean there, ate that

Spread the chia pudding thin on a platter to create a soccer field, football field, or other sports arena. Mold the donuts into different shapes for different types of balls. Post your creation on social media using the hashtag #beansproutskitchen.

(continued)

FOR THE DONUT HOLES:

⅓ cup (87 g) creamy nut, seed, or soy butter

½ cup (115 g) packed brown sugar

1 egg

2 tablespoons (30 g) plain Greek yogurt

⅓ cup (80 ml) milk (of your choice)

1 teaspoon pure vanilla extract

¾ cup (94 g) flour

¼ cup (28 g) ground flax meal

1 teaspoon baking powder

¼ teaspoon salt

FOR THE GLAZE:

¾ cup (90 g) powdered sugar

1½ tablespoons (30 g) raspberry preserves

1½ tablespoons (25 ml) milk (of your choice)

YOU WILL ALSO NEED:

Hand blender

Mini muffin tin

Mini cupcake liners

Child scissors

Paper

Colored pencils or pens

Scotch tape

Toothpicks

To make the Donut Holes-in-One:

1. Preheat oven to 350°F (180°C).

2. In a large bowl, use a hand blender to mix the nut, seed, or soy butter and brown sugar, about 3 to 4 minutes. Blend in the egg, yogurt, milk, and vanilla extract.

3. In a small bowl, mix the flour, flax meal, baking powder, and salt. Fold the dry ingredients into the wet mixture just until blended.

4. In a mini muffin tin lined with cupcake liners, divide the batter among the liners. Bake for 10 to 12 minutes. Let cool slightly. While still warm, squish up each mini muffin in your hands and roll until it becomes a circle.

5. Stir the powdered sugar, raspberry preserves, and milk together in a small bowl. Lightly glaze the donut holes and place on a piece of parchment paper until set.

6. Use child scissors to cut 20 little triangles from the paper and create your own little flags using colored pencils. Tape each one to a toothpick.

7. Place your flagstick on top of each donut hole and place on the Pudding Greens.

Bean appétit!

Makes 18 to 20 Donut Holes-in-One

note

If you have a cake pop maker, feel free to use that instead when baking— it will make the donut holes more circular.

ACKNOWLEDGMENTS

A big "sprout out" to:

- Mr. Steffes' art class
- Our Pea Brains—Beth, Colin, Jessica, and Carrie
- The amazing taste testers—the Cork, Earp, Hall, Hedger, Kozicky, Lawton, Matthews, Mildwoff, Newton, Patch, Rawhouser, Rohlfs, Tucker, and Yanke families
- Peafessor Hoyt
- Grandma Bean
- Lilly and the Full Circle Literary team
- The editorial Pod Squad at The Quarto Group
- Our Pretty Peas: Laura and Annie
- Our true MVPeas: all of our Bean Team employees who work so hard to bring our vision to reality
- Our Bean Stock families: Adamschecks, Allens, Andersons, Baileys, Bobkos, Butlers, Chandlers, Ciurczaks, Farnsworth/Wallers, Furdas, Giogas, Gonsalves, Grainges, Guenthers, Hillcoats, Jankowskis, Kellys, Klafters, Littles, Moaks, Nakalsaacs, Pokempners, Polazzis, Preheims, Rawhausers, Rogers, Rome/Kielpikowskis, Roushs, Schaefers, Simpsons, Warrens, Williams/Bennetts, Witts, Wolfes, Yokums, and Zohars
- Bean Sprouts' family destination partners
- The Payette and Kaminski families for their neverending support and enthusiasm
- Our sweetest peas: Isaac, Bini, Adrian, and Roger, and Kale, Makena, and Eric

ABOUT THE AUTHORS

Shannon "Peacasso" Seip and Kelly "Pea Brain" Parthen are the co-founders of Bean Sprouts, a hip and healthy café chain that focuses on families. By planting their cafés in high-profile family destinations (like museums, science centers, zoos, and tourist attractions), Bean Sprouts is in front of more than 8 million visitors annually.

Shannon and Kelly are touted as experts in making healthy food fun and have been recognized multiple times as "movers and shakers" in the restaurant industry. They visited the White House to meet with Michelle Obama's Let's Move! team to discuss Bean Sprouts' role as an innovative leader in the food service industry. They are featured speakers at major industry conferences from Association of Children's Museums (ACM) and Association of Science & Technology Centers (ASTC) to Fast Casual Executive Summit and International Association of Amusement Parks & Attractions (IAAPA).

Their first cookbook, *Bean Appétit: Hip & Healthy Ways to Have Fun with Food*, debuted when they had just one café. *Bean Appétit* was named one of the Top 10 Kids' Cookbooks by iVillage (now today.com) and has been featured on *The Today Show*, *Good Morning America*, and in nearly every major parenting publication and website. Shannon has written several additional books, including two for American Girl and was a top-ranked contributing editor of NickMom/Nickelodeon, both online and on air.

Bean our guest and visit beansprouts.com for more information.

INDEX

ALSO AVAILABLE

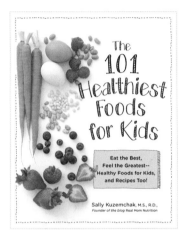

The 101 Healthiest Foods for Kids

978-1-59233-848-1

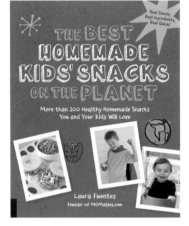

The Best Homemade Kids' Snacks on the Planet

978-1-59233-661-6

The Best Homemade Kids' Lunches on the Planet

978-1-59233-608-1